We Are Made of Found Objects
© 2015 JM Romig
PHP#10
Poets' Hall Press
Erie, Pennsylvania
ISBN 978-0-9766929-6-6

Third Printing. Licensed with author's
permision to Beautiful Blasphemy
beautifulblasphemypoetry@gmail.com

Cover Art: © Amanda Whitlock

We Are Made of Found Objects

JM Romig

Winner of the 2015 Chapbook Contest
sponsored by
The Erie County Poet Laureate

Acknowledgements

For Danielle, my amazing wife, private editor
and harshest critic; for Ryan, who dragged me
to my first "real" poetry reading; and for all the
English teachers over the years who asked me
to send them a copy of my first collection. I
don't have any of your addresses. I hope this
dedication suffices.

Contents

We are Made of Found Objects

He is a makeshift scarecrow
filled with crumpled up first drafts
of love notes
kicked through cobwebs that linger
in the long forgotten corners
of old classrooms.

She is an island of kindling –
bits and pieces
of broken bottles, crumpled newspaper
and other misplaced things tossed out
into the ocean
forced to swim, wet
and freezing, forever gathering
to form a huddled mass of leftovers
longing to be set on fire.

They are a collage of poorly taken Polaroids
of strangers
in waiting rooms
with fingers knotted in prayer
or tedium –
held together by masking tape and pushpins
on a well-loved corkboard

I am a tightly sealed mason jar
full of captive fireflies,
pillbugs, caterpillars and moss
and not enough air holes in my lid.

I fear these things will die inside of me.

and you,
you, too, are a mason jar
but you are full of brightly colored
off-brand jellybeans
with a thick black question mark
painted on your face.

Thoughts, Like Fireflies
in the Night Sky

The only thing I like
about nights like this
is that it gets so dark
and the skies are so clear
that they look like
the little boy who trapped us all here
decided to have mercy
and pin-prick little tiny airholes
in the lid of our mason jar

but there aren't enough
to make a difference

Her lit cigarette burns
so brightly from the porch
against the darkness
it reminds me of a lighthouse
. . . or a bug zapper.

I don't see how anyone
can smoke at a time like this
when the air is so heavy
it's like breathing cement.

The campfire is whispering
something about . . . memories?
I can't hear it very well
and I don't speak its language.

The fireflies are out tonight.
I watch the children chasing them
as they blink in and out of existence
like little teleporting fairies –
Proof that the little boy who trapped us all here
has not yet succeeded
in snuffing out all of the magic.

One child is sitting away from the group
swinging alone
carving imperfect circles
with her toes
into the dirt below.
She is staring up at the stars
she looks – concerned.
I cannot help but
wonder what she's thinking.

The campfire is dying.
I watch it gasp for air a few last times
before putting it out of its misery.

Wandering About Campus – Early Spring

I hear a voice of a guitar –
the chords to an Irish jig –
Whisky in the Jar.
I stand there a moment
listening hard and rocking softly.

I am not sure if it's just the weight of winter
finally melting off my shoulders,
or if there's something deeper,
something spiritual happening here.

I take a nice long breath of the Ohio air,
feeling relief, release, and repair.

Two Hours Till Kentucky

The world is on fast-forward around us
The side of my forehead is flat
against the passenger side window
Trees crowd behind guardrails for miles –
protesting highway pollution.

Two hours till Kentucky –
On the eighth round about this CD.
About around the fifth listen, songs began to blend
into one another, morphing into ambient noise
that filled the empty moments between conversation
and the struggle against waves of tempting sleep.

Two hours till Kentucky–
I pause the song to explain
the biographical significance
of a particular lyric.
You're too focused on
the nerve-wracking traffic to indulge me.

Two hours till Kentucky–
My seat reclined, I am watching the clouds
creeping briskly across the sky
through the panorama of the windshield –
a silent movie.

Two hours till Kentucky –
an eternity of moments
gone as soon as they happen.
Evaporating into the air

We'll be there
in no time

The Wishing Well Tattoo

There's this tattoo I wish to get
if I ever get rid of this fear
of making decisions.

It's this little girl, maybe seven years old or so
she's holding on to an aged dandelion by its neck.
Her eyes are closed and open to a whole other world –
she shoots a wish toward it
with every muscle in the body
that she doesn't know yet.

The seeds are propelled across my back
and transform into the shooting stars they
always dreamed they'd be.
Somewhere below
on an otherwise empty beach
are a couple of teenagers
discovering themselves inside one another.
They kiss and tell no one.
The blanket promises to keep their secret
and the sand sneaks into places it knows
it's unwelcome.

They are drunk on the passion of the moment.
She's lost in the stars
and wants to gently scoop those lights from the sky
seal them in a mason jar
and watch them do their cosmic dance around each other
to remind herself of how small she feels under them
and how amazing it felt to be everything
and nothing at the same time.
She holds her breath, closing her eyes
sending up a wish in the music of young lust.

Meanwhile,
on my rightmost shoulder blade
There's an older man, looking down a wishing well
at the two young lovers' play.

Smiling at his memories which, like the ink, are fading.
A wish falls out of his mouth and speeds down into the
        darkness
it bounces off the back of the boy's head,
and is gobbled up by the greedy sand.

Hospice

Her eyes are so deep set now
that in a certain light
they are just holes in her face

She is so thin now
from the chemotherapy
her skin seems little more than
an empty balloon stretched over her skeleton
and tied off at the scalp,
to keep what's left of her from falling out

She shakes so bad now
that she needs assistance
to cease the drought
on the jagged landscape of her lips

Now, her days are spent
in an endless sleep
punctuated by a waking sleep
in which she does a lot of staring at walls
and vomiting

That waking sleep, or living nightmare,
is itself punctuated by the occasional friend
come to mourn at the gravemarker
that is her hospital bed
She now has sympathy for the zombie
knowing what it's like to be dead
and alive at the same time

She thinks, if she had the energy,
she might bite people too
just to remind them
that she's still here

Short Poems
About Our New Neighbors

Across the court yard
The amorous twenty-somethings
Open their window for the first time

They let the sun shine in –
They do not believe in curtains –
They let the sunshine in

He is Adonis
She is Mona Lisa
I hate them so much

It's five in the morning
Our child screams us awake
Meanwhile, they sleep until noon

Passing by the window
I glimpse at the lovers entwined
"Not tonight" you yawn

Our friends are laughing
About what, we cannot tell
All we see is their love

He brings her breakfast in bed
Maybe it's a birthday present? I suggest
Or he screwed up, bigtime – you reply cynically

They've become background noise
Only witnessed in passing
Or referenced in our idle conversation

A few weeks have passed
Their room is empty and still
We almost forget they were ever there

She sits on her bed and stares at nothing
She has not moved for hours –
A lonely still life

Adonis is waning
His eyes are sinking, and he's losing hair
He's become a walking skeleton

He does not move much these days
All of the time, she waits by his side
For whatever comes next

I keep telling you
That he will soon recover
I have to believe this

He's sitting up today
Telling jokes and laughing,
She's cracking that famous smile

The room is now full
With what must be family and friends
Saying their goodbyes

She is being cradled
by, I think, her mother – or aunt
We weep along

The guests are now long gone
The silence settles like dust
She holds his hand while he fades

Soon, it will be just her (and us)
Left in this quiet room
Alone

On Meeting Ted Kooser

He sat there behind the table,
with his glasses sitting on his nose,
and his skin sitting on his bones – both loosely,
the way you'd expect someone to sit
after 75 years of good, but hard, living.

"The trick is–" he said
deliberately pausing to shift the weight of the sentence
toward the upcoming words
"you have to wipe away all the things you don't want to see."
He said this as he scribbled his name
inside my new copy of his old book
smiling in that gentle old man way.

I scampered away like a schoolboy
feeling like an idiot
having rambled at him
in my best impression of a scholar
– like a kid wearing his dad's oversized suit.

I talked at him about
how well he captures a moment in poetry
like this former US Poet Laureate
wasn't aware of his talent
and I was somehow the first
delivering the good news.

As I wander the campus,
having escaped my embarrassment
I think back to a poem he read tonight
about watching an old couple sharing a sandwich.

It was an ode to love,
an image you can see in any sit-down restaurant,
literally anywhere in America.
He focused in on this couple,
in this diner
at this moment
apart from time, like a moving still life
forever framed by his words.

He wiped away the screaming kid
and its overwhelmed mother in the booth to the left,
the table of teenagers playing hooky to their right,
and the underpaid twentysomething waitress
who clearly didn't want to be there anyway.

He wiped away all of that distraction
and unearthed this beautiful moment
this pure example of true love—
A sandwich cut from corner to corner
by the shaking hands of a man
whose glasses sit upon his face
and skin upon his bones
all the way you expect a man to
with a woman he's loved for forty years
with whom he shares everything.

I think about the moments I have missed
the poems never writ
because I was staring at the waitress,
who clearly didn't want to be there anyway.

#TRNT
In Memory of Gill Scott Heron

The revolution will not be televised.
The revolution will not be televised.
The revolution will not be televised.
The revolution will be live—

streaming through your Windows
laptops and smartphones.
The revolution will be blogged,
tweeted, liked, shared, RE-blogged RE-tweeted
and Stumbled Upon in between
midnight masturbation sessions
sandwiched between funny cat memes.

The resolution will be HD.
Its evolution will be high speed.
The whistles will be blown at with frequency.
The revolution will be commented on;
Scrutinized.
Vandalized.
Scandalized.
Stylized and advertised.
People will pay attention –
People will forget to mention
that some stand up, occupy, riot
and die.

The revolution will not be televised.
The revolution will be streaming live
through the filter of your choice.

The facts will be democratized.
The democracy will be corporatized.
The corporations will be personified.
People, objectified –
Spied on and villainized
The powers that be will lie, deny, and try to justify.
The people will be disenfranchised.
Prisons will be privatized.
Death drones will be utilized.

No one will bat an eye.
Because the revolution will be multiplied, over-simplified,
The violence, normalized.
Lives, sacrificed
to satiate the Golden Calf's appetite.

The revolution will not be televised
but Jerry Springer will. . . .
Go figure.

Ode on an Ode
To A Nightingale

Sitting in a corner booth by herself,
sipping on a Long Island Iced Tea
and reading Keats.
Hands down, she's the most
captivating person in this bar.

Fingertips calloused, and hands nicked and scraped
like she'd been in a fight with experience
and went down swinging.
Eased into her seat like slipping naked into a hot bath.
Smiled with all her teeth
like no one was looking.

Left her phone at home,
in pieces on the kitchen floor.
Tonight was the night she was going to forget all
about the custody battle
the bill collectors
the late night fights about who was right
and who was left in the room
with all this shattered glass to clean up
the long sobbing nights with her pillow
and her secret shame
the regret for time poorly spent
looking for love in bars and cold blue eyes
the years that separated her from twenty-two –
when she was young and delusionally happy.

With her body language, she unknowingly spoke to me:
Tonight, I came to drink and dance.
Don't bother me with pick up lines.
Pick up artists, go find another canvas.
Mine's been painted over plenty.
I don't have the time to save any more white knights
from their mother's tit.
That fairytale story always ends in
Shakespearean tragedy.
Plus, the damn horse leaves scuff marks on the dance floor.

I take one last sip
and slip the bartender an extra twenty—
tonight the nightingale drinks for free.

I leave before she can thank me.

Brothers

I

The phone was screaming in my pocket
its voice was muffled by the pile of clothes
on top of it

The hotel water was almost too hot
it turned my scalp red
and cascaded down my face
in a way that should have felt like baptism

After what felt like an eternity
the call went to the black hole
of my neglected voicemail
now at over a hundred missed calls

I didn't want to talk
not to Dad, not to Mom,
not to my girlfriend,
and definitely not to some reporter
trying to make our fucked-up family
the topic of the nine o'clock news

II

The pipes in the wall
clunked around for a second
as I turned the knob, cutting the water off
I stepped out of the shower
somehow feeling less clean than when I entered

For a moment I stood there,
towel over my head
in complete darkness

I closed my eyes and saw him
standing across from me
his eyes, locked with mine
dad's gun in his shaking hands –
pointed directly at my head
unblinking, full of hatred, anger
and fear

They'll call him a monster
and knowing what he's done,
I won't be able to say they're wrong

III
Sympathizers will say that the divorce
messed him up somehow
or that he inherited our mother's mental illness
or that he played too many first person shooters –

which is just fucking stupid

Lying on the hotel bed,
I nakedly examined the ceiling
mapping out the distance between water stains
like a cartographer

The last time he called me
he was in tears,
because some pricks from his school
beat him to a pulp
and shoved his face in dog shit

I can't help but dwell
on something I said to him that night:

"People like that don't change
they become asshole adults
and keep kicking people around
because they can
Because they're rich and we're poor
and they don't want to see people like us
we remind them that the world isn't perfect
and doesn't revolve around them"

I don't want to believe
that I planted the seed,
that the **one** time he listened to me –

IV
Six people died
most of them, kids no older than seventeen
one teacher, and a janitor – tagged by a stray bullet
two kids have been in critical condition
for the last three days

He must have been terrified
in those last moments
before the cops riddled him with holes

He must have regretted it
or at least regretted
not having an escape plan

He never did think things through
unlike me,
connecting the countries on the ceiling
drawing imaginary lines
of cause and effect
and trying to figure out what it means
to be a big brother
in the absence of a little one

I Was Immortal Once

I was immortal once,
believe me, you, I was
invincible.
And back when I was immortal
I used to play hopscotch on the clouds
high above New York City Traffic
and laugh every time I caught myself
on the edge.

I used to play hide and seek
with the truth

I'd hide in the bedroom closet
of this muse
and be there when
she'd come home after a long day's
inspiration.
I'd watch her undress
searching her naked self in the mirror
like something was missing
but she never did find it.
I think she knew I was there
yeah, she knew.

I used to race with shooting stars
I won once
but I cheated
so it doesn't count.

I used to dance with The Moon all night
she moved my waters
and I took her virginity.
Ours was a love of necessity.

I kissed The Sun.
She blushed
and The Moon got jealous.
Then I met God,
the most beautiful of all my conquests.
I knew no one else would quite match up to her.
She and I made a man together.
It was parenthood that tore us apart.

Yeah, I was immortal once
but now,
now I'm just waiting to die
like everyone else.

Colophon

This chapbook originally published by Poets' Hall Press, Erie, Penna. Poets' Hall Press is grateful to the Erie County Poet Laureate Initiative and especially Poet Laureate Cee Williams for supporting featured readings at Poets' Hall and helping to fund the 2015 chapbook series. This work was a winner of the 2015 chapbook contest created and funded by Laureate Williams. It was edited and arranged by Greg Brown for Poets' Hall Press. The text is set in Open Source fonts: Armalite Rifle, Carbon Type (Vic Fieger), Liberation Sans, and Liberation Serif (Red Hat).

The Original Poets' Hall, 1136 East Lake Road, Erie.

About the Author

Joshua Michael (JM) Romig was born and raised right by Lake Erie in Ashtabula, Ohio. He eventually escaped, earned a BA in English and settled down in Ravenna, Ohio. JM has made a bit of a name for himself as an avid poetry fanatic, featuring in Cleveland and Erie, as well as earning a spot as a finalist of Writing Knights' Grand Tournament Championship in 2014. He has been described by critics (*i.e.*, friends) as a "street poet," a "storyteller," and a "dude who owes me five dollars."

He wants to go on record saying he has every intention of paying that last guy back, eventually.